Praise for *Sales Optimization System*

SOS provides a series of "maps" to have a successful sales effort, and it is a comprehensive sales planning and sales activity management system.

Salespeople must manage the "metrics" of selling, as well as effectively execute every step in their sales process.

SOS provides a framework for approaching the right kind of customer and saying the right things at the right time. Strong interest getting statements, framing questions which identify real customer needs, and matching the right solutions to primary buying motivations are all housed as selling assets within SOS.

SOS helps a sales team manage sales information, as well as prospect and client information. This helps clarify what has been accomplished, and what steps are required to complete a customer agreement.

--**Jon Halleen**, Principal, Applied Humanics

Sales Optimization System

Sales Optimization System

The Life Preserver Your Sales Plan Needs

Jeff Conner

Q: How do you defeat sales reps?

A: Give them a phone

There is no magic bullet. Success is right in front of you...just do the next right thing, then the next. That is the only formula and secret to success.

---- Jeff Conner

Cover Image: Robert Simbron

Cover Design: Robert Simbron

Copyright © 2020 by Jeff Conner
All rights reserved. This book or any portion thereof may not be reproduced or used in any manner whatsoever
without the express written permission of the publisher
except for the use of brief quotations in a book review.

Printed in the United States of America

First Printing, 2020

ISBN 9798590995424

Jeffery Conner Publishing
20582 Austin St. NE
Cedar, MN 55011

www.jefferyconner.com

For Tony Emmerich- Thank you for giving me a chance.

Contents

	Forward by Barbara Zuleger	8
	Welcome!	11
	Introduction	12
1	Powerful Planning & Strategy	15
2	Accelerated Lead Generation	31
3	Obsessive Prospecting	33
4	Impactful Meetings	44
5	Decisive Demos & Proposals	57
6	Confident Closing	69
7	Purposeful Professional Development	75

Forward by Barbara Zuleger, Founder of Performance Partners Coaching

The confidence, creativity and energy of a true entrepreneur can literally create something from nothing. Jeff is a true entrepreneur leading with passion, vision, and motivation. For Jeff, building a business, whether a catering business or a non-profit to improve quality of life for others, is all consuming. He is at his finest, and happiest when developing a great business idea into a great business.

It is said that reading a book can teach you in a few short hours what it took someone else at least five years to learn. Author and creator of the *Sales Optimization System*, Jeff, is the first to admit the errors made when rushing too quickly into hiring a sales team. You will be so glad you picked up this book, you just saved yourself a lot of time, money, and anxiety. You don't have time to make the same mistakes others have made, you have your own to make.

Jeff created this system which he so thoughtfully lays out in this book because he needed to make sense of why his own sales experience and success were not translating into a successful sales team. The *Sales Optimization System* fills the gaps, between 'this is what I do' and 'this is a tool I can use over and over again to continually build the sales process, team and results I need in my small business'.

> *Entrepreneurs start businesses. Business owners run businesses.*
> *Smart entrepreneurial business owners build a team to run the daily operations in their business.*

Successful business leaders need to spend less time in day-to-day operations so they can focus on keeping their business on the leading edge. This may be the leading edge in a huge industry like a Steve Jobs, or it may mean a successful owner of a small to mid-size business staying on the leading edge in their community.

When I first met Jeff, in 2013, he was new to this world of small business. He gave me a challenge I see consistently when working with my business builder clients, that is, getting him to slow down enough to see the whole business. Jeff doesn't have a slow-down mode, and he did not want to look at the whole business, the business was fine, all he needed was help with marketing.

Marketing, while essential, was not the only thing that needed attention in this business. Jeff's goal was to be a Leveraged Business Owners as quickly as possible. Leveraged business owners need a team they can depend on.

Jeff knew how to talk to customers about his amazing product, and how to help them buy, aka selling. But in a business that was set to grow quickly, it was not where his time and talent was best utilized. He was needed as the CEO not out selling the product. Building a sales team in a business that has never had a successful one is not a one-step process. Hiring an experienced salesperson is not enough to get great results. Great salespeople sell. Setting up the sales process and all that entails requires a different set of skills and experience.

> *"When I hired my first sales reps, I didn't have a system for them. I thought I could just hire a sales rep and they would "just figure it all out." This turned out to be a huge mistake and cost me several thousand dollars and about six months of time. You see, great sales reps don't want to develop a system, they want to sell."* Sales Optimization System

You can do this! Sales Optimization System is a detailed, robust, and straightforward system to help small business owners develop a strong sales process and build a team to implement that process. Not an expert in sales? New to building a sales team? Great this system was created for you.

Sales are not the only important component in a healthy business, you cannot have a healthy business without it. Congratulations on making the commitment to learning all you can about creating a strong, consistent sales process, hiring the sales team that can implement it, and helping them continue to grow, because this is the only way your business can give you the quality of life you have dreamed of.

Barbara Zuleger, Business Strategist and Coach
Founder of Performance Partners

Sales Optimization System

Welcome!

Congratulations on taking your first step toward creating your world class sales program. The Sales Optimization System is designed to give you step by step instructions to implement a sales process for your company. Once you've implemented these steps, you will have the structure you need for a world class sales process giving you the ability to create predictable and repeatable sales results.

The modules of the Sales Optimization System are:

- *Powerful Planning and Strategy*
    - *Creating and documenting the sales process*
    - *Setting up the Customer Relationship Manager (CRM)*
    - *Documented Job Descriptions*
    - *Setting KPI's and Report Templates*
- *Accelerated Lead Generation*
- *Obsessive Prospecting*
- *Impactful Meetings*
- *Decisive Demos and Proposals*
- *Confident Closing*
- *Purposeful Professional Development*

Here's to your sales success!

Jeff Conner

Sales Optimization System

Introduction

The Sales Optimization System, or SOS, has been developed through years of trial and error as I created the sales system, we use at my catering company and with our coaching and consulting company, Performance Partners.

When I hired my first sales reps, I didn't have a system for them. I thought I could just hire a sales rep and they would "just figure it all out." This turned out to be a huge mistake and cost me several thousand dollars and about six months of time. You see, great sales reps don't want to develop a system, they want to sell. Sales professionals want a system to work within, but they don't want to create it for you. Not only do they not want to do it, but they most likely don't have the skills to do it. There is a big difference in the skills required to sell and the skills required to build and manage a selling process and team.

I ended up letting both of our initial sales reps go within six months because I hadn't done the upfront work that would allow them to be successful. Without a clearly documented system, they didn't understand my expectations and I couldn't hold them accountable for getting results. It turned out to be a tremendous waste of resources and their time.

After letting them go, I did what I should have done first, I created a sales program. Once I had my program in place, I then hired two new sales reps and am happy to say they are both doing extraordinary selling for us and have helped us double our revenue in just a few years.

Sales Optimization System works!

I'm thrilled to share what I've learned with you.

The SOS program is designed to take you from wherever you are currently in your sales development to having a complete program to manage your sales professionals and sales team. It gives you, the owner, the ability to effectively lead and manage the sales functions at your company.

Because this is written for you, the busy owner and entrepreneur, I have left out all the fluff and get straight to the point by giving you the steps you need to take to establish a sales system for your company. You won't be wasting a lot of time reading about things you don't care about.

Implementing the SOS program is simple, but not easy. The process is straight-forward, but requires considerable time and effort to implement. If you are self-implementing, you will want to be sure you give yourself plenty of time to work on each section.

This system works, so don't give up on it! If you are having trouble with self-implementation, I'm here to help.

Visit www.salesoptimizationsystem.biz for more information and incredible resources to help you develop your sales plan. You can also contact me if you need help implementing for your business.

Jeff@jefferyconner.com

You can be ready to hire your first sales rep in as little as 30 days!

Powerful Planning & Strategy

Document the Sales Process

Powerful Planning & Strategy

Document the Sales Process

A few definitions to get us started. It doesn't matter whether you use these definitions or create your own. What does matter is that you define each of these and stay consistent with your use of these terms within your organization.

Lead Generation
- Lead: a contact on a list that may or may not be qualified
- Goal: turn leads into prospects

Prospecting
- Prospect: a contact who is in the sales pipeline and is in the process of being qualified
- Goal: move leads up prospect pyramid to become customers

Meetings
- Meetings & Conversations: scheduled two-way conversations: in-person, over the phone or online via platforms like Zoom
- Goal: develop rapport, qualify, learn needs and gain information on selling

Demos/Proposals
- Demos & Proposal: sharing information with clients on how your features match up with their needs. Introduce pricing
- Goal: Provide information to help prospect become a customer

Closed Deal
Won: Congratulations!   Lost: Move to marketing funnel
- Goal: Confirm sale, create good feelings and provide next steps

Powerful Planning & Strategy

Setting Up Your CRM

CRM- Customer Relationship Manager

Key Uses:
Create Sales Pipeline
Monitor Sales Team Performance
Contact Info
Log Emails
Log Phone Calls
Schedule Meetings
Create Notes with Relevant Information
Assign Tasks to Ensure Follow-Up
Create and Track Deals

The Sales Optimization System uses the FREE version HubSpot and all instructions pertain to setting up and using HubSpot as your CRM. If you have a CRM already, or want to use a different CRM, no problem, you can skip this section or use it to help guide you as you set up a different CRM.

Powerful Planning & Strategy

Setting Up Your CRM

STEP 1: Go to www.hubspot.com and sign up for the FREE version.

- Click the button "Get free CRM"

STEP 2: Answer Questions and Go Through the Demo

STEP 3: Set up your HubSpot account
- A. Customize your deal stages.
    - i. Click the link 'Customize deal stages'
    - ii. Customize your deal stages & assign win probability percentages
        1. Appointment Scheduled*
        2. Appointment Held
        3. Demo/Proposal Scheduled*
        4. KDM Evaluating
        5. Contract Sent
        6. Closed Won
        7. Closed Lost
    - optional pipeline stages that allow you to track no-shows for appointments and demos

Go back to Set up your HubSpot account page

- B. Import your contacts

      i. Click "Import your data" button
      ii. Click "Import" button at top of new screen
      iii. View "How to prepare your spreadsheet"
      iv. Prepare your spreadsheet as directed
      v. Click "Start an Import" button at top left
      vi. Choose "File from computer" then click Next
      vii. Choose "One File" then click Next
      viii. Choose "One object" then click Next
      ix. Choose "Contacts" then click Next
      x. Upload prepared spreadsheet
      xi. Click Next
      xii. Choose Columns and match fields

C. Connect your inbox (allows email tracking)
      i. Click the "Connect your Inbox" button
      ii. Follow instructions based on email type

D. Invite members of your team as appropriate

You now have the basic setup complete which allows you to:
- manage contacts
- create relevant notes on contacts
- track and log emails
- log phone conversations
- set follow-up tasks
- manage and monitor deals through the sales pipeline

There are many other features, such as a meeting scheduler that is synched with your calendar. This provides a link that contacts can click to get access to your availability, making scheduling appointments much easier. This is a free service.

There is also an integration for your phone number. You can record calls straight into your CRM so you can keep all your conversations in one place. This is a fee-based service.

Powerful Planning & Strategy

Job Descriptions

A complete job description for your sales representatives is essential to their success, and ultimately, to the success of your business. The job description is used to hire the best qualified candidates and to make sure they have a clear understanding of your expectations

Download a free editable Job Description at
https://www.salesoptimizationsystem.biz/resources

Below are the key considerations when developing the job descriptions for your sales force. Feel free to modify this format to fit with your existing job descriptions for other positions at your company.

- Choose a Title
    - Examples: Sales Representative, Account Manager, and Business Account Executive
    - This is your company, feel free to create your own
- Outline the reporting relationship
- Key Role with Revenue expectations based on KPIs
- Key Responsibilities

Business Account Executive

Job Description

Reporting Relationship: The Business Account Executive reports to the Sales Manager

Key Role: The BAE is responsible for selling to corporate accounts to reach sales volume of at least $15,000 per month in Corporate Drop Off and/or Event business.

Key Responsibilities:

1. Meeting or exceeding minimum sales expectation of $15,000 per month with at least a 50% margin on each event/drop off.
2. Making cold calls to schedule 3-5 Corporate Tastings per week and maintaining pipeline full.
3. Following procedures to conduct Corporate Tastings
4. Work with Marketing Manager to make recommendations on needed marketing materials.
5. Contacting, following up and maintaining contact with leads provided by the company
    a. Personal emails
    b. Constant Contact Campaigns
    c. Customer Visits
6. Lead Generation & Prospecting through cold calling, networking, social media or any other method to meet minimum sales goals and maintain pipeline at standard levels in each area.
7. Ensure proper procedures are followed to ensure each lead, contact and event is documented per company policy.
8. Procure two (2) new venues as either a Preferred Caterer or Exclusive Caterer status each 12 months.
    a. All corporate leads for venues procured by BAE will belong to that BAE and normal commission rates will apply.
    b. All Wedding/Social leads will be given to the appropriate Wedding/Social Sales Professional and the BAE will receive a 2.5% Finders Fee Commission for those events
    c. All Corporate Event Leads for a venue that is assigned to a Wedding/Social Sales Professional will be given to a BAE on a rotating basis and commission will be paid at 7.5% (the Wedding/Social Sales Professional will receive a 2.5% finders fee)
    d. These percentages outlined in b and c above are subject to change based on negotiated venue fees to be paid.
9. Maintain a score of 90% or greater for customer satisfaction with the Sales Rep and Overall Event Performance
10. Coordinate with Operations Department to ensure each event is executed per our agreement with the Customer. This means making sure the Operations Department can fulfill your promises to your customer prior to making the promise.
11. Constant education and learning to keep up with industry trends to offer the best services and value to our customers.
12. Report Key Performance Indicators to the Sales Manager weekly.
13. Complete Commission report for prior months event/drop revenue
14. Attend meetings as deemed necessary by management.

Job Descriptions

Get your FREE editable Job Description at
https://www.salesoptimizationsystem.biz/resources

Powerful Planning & Strategy

Key Performance Indicators and Reports

Key Performance Indicators (KPIs) along with the job description, are used to provide expectations and feedback to both you and your sales representative on actual results. You use these as a method of accountability to ensure your sales reps are meeting their key activity objectives and closing enough business.

The KPI Excel File is completed each week by the Sales Rep and sent to the Sales Manager. The file itself provides reporting for:
- Daily & Weekly Results
- Monthly Results
- Quarterly Results
- Current Sales Ratios and averages

Get your FREE KPI Tracker at
https://www.salesoptimizationsystem.biz/kpi-landing-page

Key Performance Indicators and Reports

Sample View of KPI and Reports

Name :-

Instructions: In each box, enter the number of occurances and your score will tally at the bottom - PLEASE do NOT enter zero's ...

Week 1

Activity	Goal	Monday	Tuesday	Wednesday	Thursday	Friday	TOTAL
Contacts Made	100	23	20	15	29	18	105
Proposals/Tours	20	4	2	1	7	8	22
Full Service Events Booked ($2500)	10	3	3	0	0	3	9
Full Service Revenue Booked	$10,000.00	3600	4000			9000	16600
							0
							0
							0
							0
							0
							0
							0
							0
	10130						0
		Sub 3600	4000	0	0	9000	16600
Week Total ...				16600			

Conversion Rates

Outside Proposals to Contacts	20%		21%
Outside Bookings to Contacts	10%		9%
Average Revenue per Event	$ 2,000.00		$ 1,844

Key Performance Indicators and Reports

Each KPI file is used by an individual sales rep for each quarter. As you can see in the image below, there are tabs for each of the three months of the quarter and a tab for the overall quarterly results.

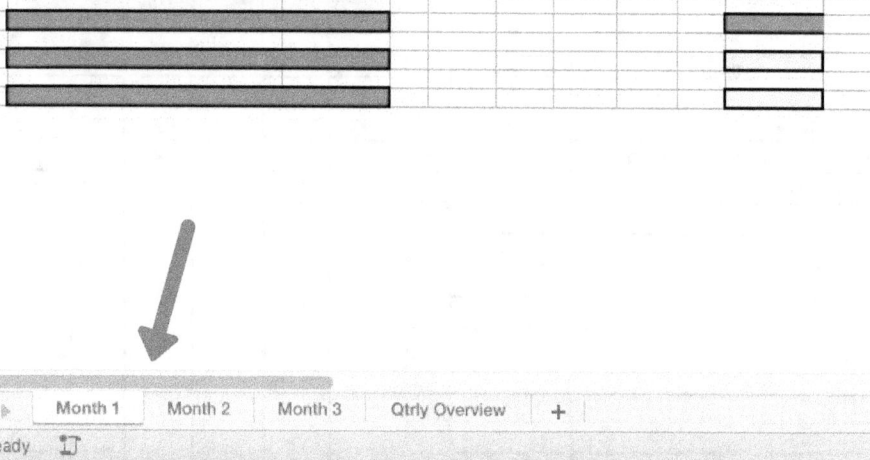

You can rename each tab to correspond to the actual months. For instance, Month 1 could change to January, or April when using strict calendar quarters.

Key Performance Indicators and Reports

Each Monthly tab shows the daily results, weekly results and total monthly results. These results are then used to fill in the results on the quarterly tab:

			Month 1					Month 2					Month 3				
Activity	Goal	Pts	Week 1	Week 2	Week 3	Week 4	Week 5	Month Tot	Week 5	Week 6	Week 7	Week 8	Week 9	Month Tot	Week 9	Week 10	Week 11	Week 12	Week 13	Month Tot	Qtr Total
Contacts Made	100		105	99	102	106	0	412	107	101	102	106		416	105	99	102	106		412	1240
Proposals/Tours	20		22	26	27	20	0	95	21	29	27	20		97	22	26	27	20		95	287
Events Booked	10		9	13	16	4	0	42	12	15	16	4		47	9	13	16	4		42	131
Revenue Booked	24000		16600	17200	18800	10000	0	62600	18100	19800	17300	10000		65200	16600	17200	17300	10000		61100	188900
Week Total	24130				62600			62600						65200				61100		61100	188900
Conversion Rates																					
Outside Proposals to Contacts	20%							23%						23%						23%	23%
Outside Bookings to Contacts	10%							10%						11%						10%	11%
Average Revenue per Event	$2,000.00							$1,490						$1,387						$1,455	$5,442

Your Sales Reps will fill in their KPI Tracker each week and submit it to you. This is your report of their results to date for each time period: daily, weekly, monthly and quarterly.

The data from the KPIs will inform commissions, awards, recognition and accountability improvement plans.

Key Performance Indicators and Reports

I've provided a free KPI Template for you. You only need to update the milestones to fit your organization.

Download your FREE KPI Template at
https://www.salesoptimizationsystem.biz/kpi-landing-page

Accelerated Lead Generation

Lead Generation:

- <u>Lead</u>: a contact on a list that may or may not be qualified

- <u>Goal</u>: turn leads into prospects

Leads are people who may or may not know about you and you don't know anything about them.

The Sales Rep uses these lists of people to create prospects.

Your company can either provide leads to sales reps or require them to find their own leads. This is up to you and what is best for your business. The important thing right now is to identify how your company and your Sales Reps will find their leads.

- How to Get Leads (RBN):
    - **R**esearching- LinkedIn, Associations, Job site boards
    - **B**uying Lists
    - **N**etworking

- Take a moment right now and identify how your organization will obtains leads

Obsessive Prospecting

Prospecting

Prospect: a contact who is in the sales pipeline and is in the process of being qualified

Goal: move leads up prospect pyramid to become customers

Sales Reps should "prospect" their leads list. The below pyramid shows the levels that prospects go through as they move toward becoming a customer

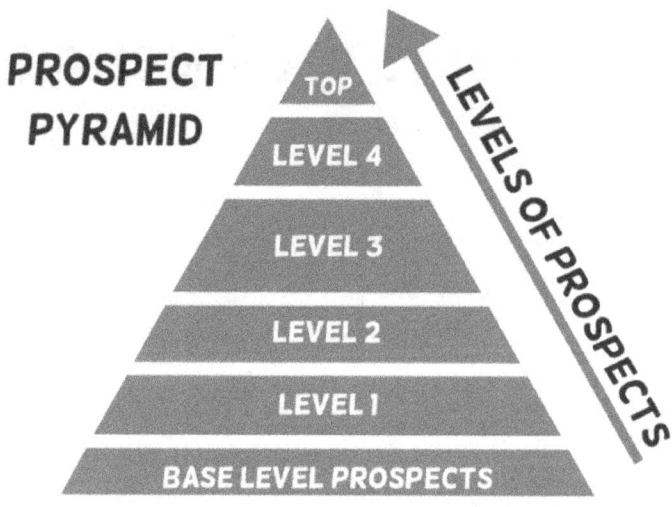

Obsessive Prospecting

BASE
Description: new Leads from BRN activities
Goal: make contact and confirm info

LEVEL 1
Description: verified contact info, understand some basic information about them
Goal: identify buying window, KDMs and influencers

LEVEL 2
Description: buying window, complete contact info, KDMs and influencers known
Goal: nurturing campaigns and regular touches to stay at top of mind

LEVEL 3
Description: targeted list of opportunities hand-picked as ideal clients
Goal: Verify qualified to buy; nurturing campaigns and regular contacts

LEVEL 4
Description: inbound leads and referrals
Goal: immediate contact to qualify and learn KDMs, influencers and buying window

TOP
Description: fully qualified to buy and in the buying window
Goal: turn into customers

Obsessive Prospecting

Sales Representatives should plan the priorities of their calls and contacts based on the prospecting pyramid. Contacts should be constantly moving up the pyramid until they close or are found to be unqualified to buy.

Prospects will often decline outright, or choose to do business with a competitor. If you provide a product and/or service that renews, wears out or can be otherwise changed or upgraded, make sure you use tasks in the CRM to follow-up on significant dates such as birthdays, anniversaries and moving into the buying window. This puts you in a place to unseat your competitor at some future point in time.

Follow-up is critical to sales success. See image for some staggering statistics. As a sales manager, spot checking contacts in your CRM to monitor follow-ups by your sales reps is critical. You don't want to waste money generating leads only to have your sales reps stop too soon!

SALES STATISTICS

48% OF SALES PEOPLE NEVER FOLLOW UP WITH A PROSPECT
25% OF SALES PEOPLE MAKE A SECOND CONTACT AND STOP
12% OF SALES PEOPLE ONLY MAKE THREE CONTACTS AND STOP
ONLY 10% OF SALES PEOPLE MAKE MORE THAN THREE CONTACTS
2% OF SALES ARE MADE ON THE FIRST CONTACT
3% OF SALES ARE MADE ON THE SECOND CONTACT
5% OF SALES ARE MADE ON THE THIRD CONTACT
10% OF SALES ARE MADE ON THE FORTH CONTACT
80% OF SALES ARE MADE ON THE FIFTH TO TWELFTH CONTACT

Source: National Sales Executive Association

When planning to make touches by phone, email, social media or in-person, Sales Representatives should start scheduling these touches with contacts at the top of the Prospecting Pyramid and work down from there as their schedule allows.

Methods of Prospecting

There are many methods to prospecting and some are more effective than others. Here is a list of methods in no particular order
- Phone calls
- Emails
- Social Media- Facebook, LinkedIn, Instagram, Twitter, etc
- In Person

Prospecting is the act of looking for deal opportunities among leads and current prospects. Now is a good time to talk about the difference between your marketing/promotion and selling activities.

Marketing/Promotion activities are geared toward getting you leads. Mass emails and social media campaigns are effective ways to generate leads.

Prospecting is the intentional act of connecting directly with a lead or prospect with the objective of moving them up the Prospecting Pyramid.

For our purposes, using email and social media for prospecting means connecting with a specific lead or prospect with the intent to qualify them, have a sales conversation and ultimately move them to customer status.

For business to business sales, one of the most effective and efficient ways to prospect is through the telephone.

Phone prospecting is commonly referred to as "cold calling". What makes cold calling so effective is you can contact more prospects in a shorter amount of time than with in-person prospecting and you have a greater chance of getting the prospects attention than through social media and email.

No matter the type of prospecting you do, it's beneficial to have a script of what you will say to get a prospect's attention and get them to commit to taking the next step, whether that's the sale, a meeting, a demo or whatever. Your goal when prospecting is to get the prospect to take another step toward becoming your customer.

Scripts should have a basic formula, but since each sales rep is different, they should be tailored to reflect the personality of the individual reps. Reps need to feel confident in their script, or the prospects will see right through them.

Prospecting Script Framework and Examples

When calling, you are interrupting the other person, so be brief and to the point. You are only an interruption if you don't provide value. If you are able to provide value in the form of creating interest, then you are no longer an interruption. Same rules apply to email, social media messaging and in-person.

Be brief and to the point so they can say yes or no and move on with their other work. Keep your commitment objective in mind before calling or emailing.

A Commitment Objective is the next step you want your prospect to commit to from this engagement. This varies depending on where the prospect is on the pyramid and in the sales pipeline. It could be you want them to commit to a meeting, to a proposal or demo, or to getting the other key decision makers in a meeting. The ultimate commitment objective is the purchase.

Approach these calls with enthusiasm and confidence. Always suggest one day and time, don't put out more than one. Also, don't ask what's best for their schedule. Confidently ask for what you want and when you want it.

If they are interested and not available at the time you suggest, they will let you know, and you can pick another day and time that works for you both. Use the following structure when crafting your phone calls, email, social media outreach or in-person visits.

Turn the page for the outline structure and sample scripts.

Structure for Prospecting Script

1. Get their attention
2. Identify yourself
3. Tell them what you want
4. Bridge to because
5. Ask for what you want

1. Get their attention
   a. Hi, Brenda…
      i. Saying their name is the best way to get their attention
   b. When you don't know their name, this is a good approach
      i. Hi, I'm calling to shamelessly promote myself and Performance Partners coaching…
      ii. Sounds corny, yes, but it gets their attention and usually gets a great smile. This works really effectively when doing in-person prospecting.
      iii. Never ask them, "How are you?"
2. Identify yourself
   a. My name is Jeff Conner and I'm with Performance Partners Coaching
3. Tell them what you want
   a. The reason for my call is I'd like to schedule a meeting with you…
   b. The reason for my email is I'd like to invite you to our upcoming webinar
   c. The reason for my call is I'd like to invite you to take our assessment

4. Bridge to because
    a. Studies have shown that acceptance rates skyrocket when you give a reason after stating "because"
        i. This isn't about you, it's about them. Avoid saying things like:
            1. "I want to talk to you about my product."
            2. "I'd love to meet with you to show you what I have to offer."
            3. "I want to tell you about our new service."
        ii. Instead, try statements like these, with "because"
            1. "Because I'd like to learn more about your unique situation and share with you some ideas that have helped our other clients
            2. "Because I'd like to share some best practices that other companies in your industry are using too..."
5. Ask for what you want… then be silent!
    a. "How about we meet on Thursday, November 14th at 1PM?
    b. "Why don't I send you the link for our assessment right now?
    c. "Can I ask you a few questions?"

Download my Cold Calling Guide and sample scripts by going to the SOS Resource page at:
https://www.salesoptimizationsystem.biz/resources

On the next page I've included three sample scripts to help you and your reps as you create your own cold-calling scripts.

Sample Scripts

Sample 1

Hi, Brenda, my name is Jeff Conner with Weaver Diversity. The reason for my call is I'd like to schedule a short meeting with you to learn more about your unique situation and share with you some ideas that have helped our other clients. I don't know if our assessment is right for you and I thought the best place to start would be to have a meeting. How about we meet via Zoom/Google Hangouts on Thursday, November 14th at 1PM for 30 minutes?

Sample 2

Hi, my name is Jeff Conner with Unique Dining Catering and I am calling to shamelessly promote myself and Unique Dining! The reason for my call is because I'd like to schedule a tasting with you so you can see if using our lunch catering would be right for you and your company. I don't know if we are right for you, and thought the best place to start would be our free tasting. How about we schedule 30- 45 minutes on November 15th at noon?

Sample 3

Hi Taylor, my name is Jeff Conner with Weaver Diversity and I am calling because I'd like to schedule a short meeting with you to go over the Weaver Diversity Inclusion Assessment. Many of my clients were frustrated because the assessment tools they were using didn't give them the data to help them really make a difference with their client companies. They have only been able to assess the organization or the individual, but not both. Our assessment is the only validated assessment that provides data and reporting on the organization and the individuals, giving you a leg up on helping your clients move the dial when it comes to their diversity and inclusion initiatives. I have 2PM on Thursday open, how about we get together for a short meeting so I can learn more about you and see whether it makes sense to schedule a demo?

Final Notes on Prospecting

- A key to using the script is to not pause. Go right through your script until the end when you ask for what you want. Then stop and stay silent until they respond. This is your first "sell" where you are trying to get a commitment from them for the next step in the sales process.
- Practice-Practice-Practice: you don't want to sound like you are reading a script, so you need to know it well enough for it to sound natural and conversational to the person you are giving it to.
    - Practice doesn't make perfect
    - Perfect practice makes perfect
- Remember, sales reps are individuals. Give them the liberty to develop their own scripts that fit their unique personality.
- Test and measure for effectiveness- prospecting works, whether on the phone, in-person, via email or over social media, it works and is effective.
    - Try different scripts and track their effectiveness
    - It's not about getting everyone to set an appointment, but if you could go from 1 out of 100 calls setting an appointment to 2 out of 100, you would effectively double your sales.

Impactful Meetings

Meetings & Conversations:

Meetings are where the magic happens because you show your prospect why you and your product are the best choice to solve their problem. For meetings, there should be a definite flow based on how your prospect will make a buying decision. Here are the things that prospects "buy" from you, in the order they "buy" them:

The sales person
The company
The product
The price
Sale

Before becoming a customer, your prospects make four decisions to "buy" before the sale. The first thing they buy is their sales person. Do they know, like and trust the person meeting with them? Next, they decide on whether or not your company is the right company. Then, they decide if the product and/or service will solve their problem or help them take advantage of an opportunity. Then they must decide whether there is enough value in your product to justify the price. If they "buy" all of these, then a sale should be a natural next step.

Unfortunately, many sales people just wing it and don't use a plan. Many sales reps will go right into doing a "features" dump and tell their prospects all about how great their product and company are before learning anything about what the prospect needs or wants.

This is where you can gain a huge advantage by setting up your sales process to align with the way your prospect makes buying decisions. Using this system, sales reps will start by selling themselves, then the company, followed by the product, then introduce price and finally ask for the sale.

And this might not all happen in one or even two meetings!

The first thing your sales rep is going to sell is themself. They need to become known, liked and trusted. Listening is the best way to accomplish this because it puts the prospect as the focal point, not the sales rep or the product.

The best way to listen is to ask questions. Here we don't want to ask just any questions, but we want to ask the best questions. Questions that draw out the wants and needs of the prospect.

During meetings it's important to keep the prospect talking. The rule of thumb is that the prospect should be talking 70% of the time and the sales rep 30%. As we draw out the needs of the prospect by asking questions, we want to know how and what to sell.

How to sell is answered when we know:
- Budget
- Timeline for purchase and urgency
- Competitors
- Influencers and other Key Decision Makers

What to sell is answered when we know:
- The problem the prospect is trying to solve
- The opportunity the prospect is trying to take advantage of
- The benefits the client wants to have from your product/service

The sales rep's job is to find out answers to these questions. Learning "how" to sell determines whether additional meetings with KDMs and influencers are needed and how to differentiate and create value.

Learning "what" to sell means tying your product's features to the benefits the prospect is looking to achieve.

A great example of this was a time when I watched one of my initial sales reps work with a prospective couple who was interested in booking their wedding at one of our venues. As I watched this sales rep give her tour to the couple, I noticed she jumped right into describing all of the features of our venue, catering and other services. As she walked them around the facility, she explained all the details, including an extensive explanation of our bar and liquor services and the associated packages available.

After the tour was over, it was time to sit and get down to "selling" our venue to this couple. I will never forget when they told our sales rep that they were non-drinkers and didn't want to have any alcoholic beverages at their wedding. I immediately thought about the 10 minutes or so that my sales rep spent, earlier, telling them all the features and how great our bar packages were. They must have been rolling their eyes and wondering how much the sales rep even cared about them and what they wanted.

We wasted precious time telling them about a service they didn't even want and that wouldn't benefit them in any way!

Needless to say, we didn't get that booking, but we learned a valuable lesson. Ask questions and find out what they want before telling them all about what we do. When you ask questions, you learn how to connect their wants and needs to your solutions. This builds value and when you create enough value, price becomes less important. Build enough value, and they will look for their own ways to justify the price you are asking.

Asking questions and actively listening shows your prospect that you care. This is the way to build trust and confidence and is what of the best ways to begin building differentiated value. Next, we are going to start formulating the plan for asking the best questions.

Asking Great Questions:

Questions to ask to learn HOW to sell:

- To help me hone in on what differentiates us from the competition, can you tell me who else you're considering besides us?
- To save us time and ensure I can provide you the right solution, can you tell me what your budget is?
- Who besides yourself, is involved in making this decision?
- How will a decision be made?
- How soon are you looking to make a decision?

Questions to ask to learn WHAT to sell:

Here you are trying to uncover their needs and wants. We go from broad needs to more specific needs that are focused on what's at stake for them personally.

What would you say is your company's biggest challenge?
What, in your opinion, is causing this challenge?
What would it mean to your company or you personally if this problem doesn't get solved?

The point of this type of questioning is to find out what benefits the prospect is seeking. To do this, it's helpful to understand and list out the benefits your customers get from your products. You can do this yourself, and I also recommend asking a few of your best customers what main benefits they get from you.

For SOS, we're going to identify benefits and then condense them to a list of no more than five. Then we'll use these as a basis for five very specific questions that will help you understand your prospect's needs.

How Benefits and 5 Questions Work

Example of the Top Benefits Of SOS:

- Higher revenues with predictable and repeatable sales
- Increased business valuation
- Scale your business
- Attract, hire and retain high quality sales professionals
- More time to work on your business

I show prospects this list and then ask them a series of five questions. The questions and their sequence are very important and should be followed exactly.

1. Based on your current situation, which of these is your number one priority right now?
2. Why did you pick that one?
3. Is it important to you? Why, in your case?
4. What are the consequences?
5. Does that worry you? Why?

List out the Benefits from Your Solution

1. _____

2. _____

3. _____

4. _____

5. _____

6. _____

7. _____

8. _____

Now identify your top five benefits

1._____

2._____

3._____

4._____

5._____

Use these when asking the five questions by creating a nice one-page document like found on the next page. Or, you can even print them on the back of your business card and ask the five questions when you hand out your card!

HOW THE SALES OPTIMIZATION SYSTEM WILL CHANGE YOUR BUSINESS

Top 5 Reasons Business Owners Choose SOS

1 HIGHER REVENUES WITH PREDICTABLE AND REPEATABLE SALES

2 INCREASED BUSINESS VALUATION

3 SCALE YOUR BUSINESS

4 ATTRACT, HIRE AND RETAIN HIGH QUALITY SALES PROFESSIONALS

5 MORE TIME TO WORK ON YOUR BUSINESS

LOOKING AT YOUR CAREER OR BUSINESS RIGHT NOW, WHICH OF THESE IS YOUR NUMBER ONE PRIORITY?

PERFORMANCE PARTNERS COACHING

Do this for yourself with the list of benefits to implementing SOS and see how this could work for you.

LOOKING AT YOUR CAREER OR BUSINESS RIGHT NOW, WHICH OF THESE IF YOUR NUMBER ONE PRIORITY?

Five Questions

1. What is your personal number one priority right now?

2. Why did you pick that one?

3. Is it important? Why, in your case?

4. What are the consequences?

5. Does that worry you? Why is that?

Download the SOS Benefits Infographic by going to the SOS Resource page at:
https://www.salesoptimizationsystem.biz/resources

Decisive Demos & Proposals

Recall the five buying decisions prospects make:

>The Sales Person
>The Company
>The Product
>The Price
>Sale

So far, we've only helped them make the first buying decision. If you've done a good enough job building rapport, asking questions and listening, your prospect is starting to know, like and trust you. The next steps are to start demonstrating how your company and its products will solve their problem.

Up to this point, you have done very little talking. During the next two stages, you will do most of the talking, but it will go by fairly quickly. This is where you are going to tell them why your company is a good match for them and how your product solves their problem or helps them take advantage of an opportunity.

<u>Selling Your Company</u>

Tell them how your company is a good match by answering two questions:
1. What does your company do?
    a. This is pretty straightforward and would be your elevator statement.
2. Are we a good fit?
    a. Show testimonials or tell stories of how you have solved the same problem for a different client.

Looking at your list of benefits you created earlier, make a list of clients and stories that demonstrate how you've given this benefit to others.

_____
_____
_____
_____
_____
_____
_____
_____

Selling Your Product

They've bought the sales rep and the company, now it's time to sell the product. This is where a demo and written proposal are used to highlight how the features of your product provide benefits and solves their problem.

To sell your product, you will use either a demonstration (demo), a proposal, or both. If it is helpful to show how your product/service solves problems and provides benefits, then you should incorporate a demo in your sales process. Otherwise, if no demo is required, you can go straight to the proposal.

It will be helpful to have listed out the features that apply to each benefit you listed earlier. Take a sheet of paper and draw a line down the center. On the left, write down the benefit and then next to it, write down each feature that provides that benefit. It's ok if the same features apply to more than one benefit.

Decisive Demos & Proposals

<ins>Selling Your Product</ins>

The SOS process for selling your product is to relate the features of your product/service that relate directly to the benefits the prospect has told you they are looking for with your solution.

<ins>Example</ins>:

You are selling Widget Maker 1000's and you learn, through asking great questions, your prospect, who produces and sells widgets, just landed a new client who requires a weekly supply of widgets that is beyond the current capacity of their equipment to produce. You learn they need to double their output to fulfil the needs of this client. Doing so will double their revenue, help them grow their business and allow them to expand.

The owner of this business wants to expand because the new revenue stream will allow her to hire additional staff and give her a better work/life balance so she can spend more time with her family.

The benefit the prospect is looking for is getting to spend more time with her family. The features of the WidgetMaker 1000 which apply to this are the speed of the machine, the durability of the machine and the accuracy of the machine all lead to increased output at a lower cost per widget.

Here is how to relate the features to the benefit desired and gain agreement:

"Mrs. Prospect, you said you need to double your output of widgets for a new client and this will allow you to hire staffing. One Widget Maker 1000 can more than double your current output with fewer errors and less downtime. This gives you the growth you need to hire new staff and allow you to take more time off so you can spend more time with your family. How does that sound?"

Using a demo or a proposal, the process for relating the features of your products to your prospects desires is as follows:

1. State the need you discovered
2. Relate the need to the feature(s) of your product/service
3. Show how the feature(s) give the desired benefits
4. Ask how the prospect perceives your statement

Here is a breakdown:

- State the need you discovered
    - *Mrs. Prospect, you said you need to double your output of widgets for a new client and this will allow you to hire staffing.*
- Related the need to the feature(s) of your product/service
    - *One Widget Maker 1000 can more than double your current output with fewer errors and less downtime.*
- Show how the feature(s) give the desired benefits
    - *This gives you the growth you need to hire new staff and allow you to take more time*

> *off so you can spend more time with your family.*

- Ask how the prospect perceives your statement
    - *How does that sound?*

By doing this, you are confirming what the prospect has told you and gotten them to see and agree that your solution can provide them with the benefit they desire.

You can use a proposal to go through this process with each of the benefits you've discovered.

<u>Demo Meeting Procedure</u>

1. Engage your audience
    a. Capture their attention quickly. Show the feature that solves the main problem first.
2. Don't go into more detail than necessary.
    a. Avoid over-explaining and showing features the prospect doesn't care about.
    b. Show how they can get the benefits they told you they needed.
3. Show them how it works
4. If possible, let them try it
5. Gain agreement that this solves their problem and gives them the desired benefit
6. Gain the commitment objective for a Proposal Meeting

Proposal Meeting Procedure

1. Use the Proposal Template provided by going to the SOS Resource page at: https://www.salesoptimizationsystem.biz/resources
2. Outline the features provided with the associated benefit provided on paper
3. For each feature and benefit, use the four-step process:
    a. State the need
    b. Relate the need to your feature
    c. Relate the feature to the desired benefit
    d. Check prospect's perception of solution
4. Once you've shown all deliverables, ask:
    a. *"Do you have any questions?"*
    b. If yes, listen to the question, then ask follow-up questions to clarify and possibly uncover undisclosed needs.
    c. If no, state:
        i. *"I bet you're wondering what your investment might be."*
5. Move to close the sale
    a. Summarize the features and benefits again and quote the price (you can either have a second sheet of proposal with listed pricing, or state the total price)
    b. Ask, *"How does that sound?"*
        i. Positive- Ask, *"Would you like to move forward?"*
        ii. Negative- go back to answering questions to uncover other needs

Decisive Demos & Proposals

Proposal Sample

**YOUR COMPANY
PROPOSAL FOR** _____

> The proposal for services is at the heart of an independent contractor's sales tool kit. It combines key company information, your unique selling proposition, and your knowledge of a client's needs and wants into a single document that can also serve as a basis for contract negotiations.
>
> Use this sample proposal as an outline for developing your own.
>
> To delete any shaded tips (like this one), just select the tip text and then press the spacebar.
>
> The sample content throughout this proposal includes placeholder content for you to replace with your own.

OVERVIEW

> Use the overview to provide a brief summary of the reason for the proposal, and how you can best support the client's needs. You can expand on this summary throughout the rest of the proposal.

Your Company is pleased to submit this proposal for services to support Client's Company in achieving its goals for improving customer satisfaction by providing training and post-sales support for its new order entry and fulfillment system. We have partnered with dozens of small businesses throughout the Northeast—businesses committed to improving the customer experience through convenience, accuracy of orders, and timely delivery.

The Objective

> Include a purpose statement that covers the problem and the key theme around your solution. Restate the client's needs as determined by reading their RFP or your previous interview process.

- Need #1: improve response time for customer questions
- Need #2: improve upon weaknesses in upsell/cross-sell volumes
- Need #3: rapid training for staff on new system

The Opportunity/Or Problem

> Include major points and identify the opportunity. Restate the client's project goals you identified previously (such as via RFP, interview, etc.).

- Goal #1: Train all CSRs on new system within 6 weeks of go-live date
- Goal #2: Integrate sales training with functional training on new system
- Goal #3: Monitor sales volume, return rates, and key satisfaction metrics for 6 weeks following training

The Solution

> *Include recommendations that lead to your proposed solution. Summarize what you're proposing to do and how you're going to meet the goals. You'll be able to expand on the details within the 'Our Proposal' section.*

- Recommendation #1: Recommendation # 1 statement
- Recommendation #2: Recommendation # 2 statement
- Recommendation #3: Recommendation # 3 statement

Project Deliverables

Following is a complete list of all project deliverables:

Deliverable	Description
Deliverable #1	Brief description

EXPECTED RESULTS

> *Describe the results expected from the project and why your approach will achieve those results.*

We expect our proposed solution to Client's Company's requirements to provide the following results:

Financial Benefits
- Result #1: Brief description of desired result
- Result #2: Brief description of desired result
- Result #3: Brief description of desired result

Technical Benefits
- Result #1: Brief description of desired result
- Result #2: Brief description of desired result
- Result #3: Brief description of desired result

Other Benefits

> *Use this section to describe less tangible benefits such as increased morale or improved customer satisfaction.*

Proposal Sample Continued…

PRICING

The following table details the pricing for delivery of the services outlined in this proposal. This pricing is valid for ## days from the date of this proposal.

Services Cost Category #1	Price
Item Description	$0,000.00
Total Services Category #1 Costs	$0,000.00
Services Cost Category #2	
Facilities	
License Fees	
Equipment Rental	
Training	
Travel	
Marketing	
Shipping/Handling	
Total Services Category #2 Costs	
Services Cost Category #3	
Total Services Category #3 Costs	
Total	

Sample Disclaimer: Disclaimer: The prices listed in the preceding table are an estimate for the services discussed. This summary is not a warranty of final price. Estimates are subject to change if project specifications are changed or costs for outsourced services change before a contract is executed.

Get your FREE Proposal Template at
www.salesoptimizationsytem.biz/resources

Follow Instructions on template and modify as appropriate for your business.

To use during the proposal meeting:

1. Go through pages one and two to relate the features and benefits to the prospects stated needs
2. Before going to page 3- ask, "Do you have any questions?"
3. If YES, then answer and clarify questions to uncover new needs
4. If YES and they ask about price, go to page three
5. If NO, then state, "I bet you're wondering what your investment might be." and go to page 3
6. Show them Page 3 with pricing
    a. Summarize features and benefits
    b. Ask, *"Would you like to move forward?"*
        i. DO NOT SAY ANYTHING ELSE AND WAIT FOR THE PROSPECT TO ANSWER

62% of Sales Reps do not ask for the sale, so with this as part of your process, your sales reps will outperform two thirds of their competition!

Confident Closing

Confident Closing

Closing the sale

As just stated, 62% of sales reps fail to ask for the sale, so they don't close sales as often as they should. Prospects state a major reason they don't buy is that the sales rep didn't seem interested enough and didn't ask for the sale. They don't ask for the sale because they don't have a process to do it. However, with SOS, you've just seen that asking for the sale is part of your process. Not only will you initially ask for the sale, but you'll ask again if you don't get a yes right away!

Here's how it works:
- Ask, "Would you like to move forward?"
- Sales Rep remains silent for as long as necessary until the prospect answers
- The prospect will typically give one of three responses:
    - They'll say "Yes"- Congratulations!
    - They'll stall by saying something like, "I need to think about it." or "I need to check with..."
    - They'll give you an objection

Definitions

Stall: customer is not ready, but doesn't have a concrete reason why

Objection: the customer has a reason why they aren't ready because a need wasn't discovered when you were asking questions

Handling Stalls

1. Never challenge the stall
2. Say, "I understand."
3. Restate the needs and benefits the prospect confirmed earlier
4. Ask again, "Would you like to move forward?"

After asking to close the sale a second time, if they don't say yes, they will most likely provide an objection.

Handling Objections:

Since an objection is your prospect telling you a need hasn't been discovered, when you get an objection, you go back to asking great questions.

1. Ask questions to draw out the need and discover the benefit they want
2. Summarize and confirm your understanding by asking, *"Does that sound right?"*
3. Give them a positive company statement through a story and/or testimonial.
4. Present a solution by relating their desired benefit to a key feature of your product

a. Follow-up with, "How does that sound?"
5. Update proposal and pricing as necessary
6. Ask again if they'd like to move forward
7. Handle any new stalls and/or objections in the same way.
8. Always come back to asking to move forward.

Sometimes the answer is NO, or they will continue to stall. If after you've handled stalls and answered objections, you still get NO, it's time to move on. Gain agreement on following-up, thank them and move on.

Closing the sale

Handling YES!
- Congratulations, all your hard work has paid off and you've just made the sale, now what?
- Many customers will get buyer's remorse. Use this procedure to help them after they've said yes. We'll call this:

Confirming the Sale

1. Reassure your prospect on their wise decision:
   a. "Mrs. Prospect, based on our current customers' results, you are going to be thrilled with the results you get from your new Widget Maker 1000."
2. Thank your prospect
   a. "Thank you for the opportunity to serve you and for the confidence in us. I really appreciate your business."

3. Shift their focus to the next steps
    a. Schedule delivery
    b. Set-up future training sessions
    c. Coordinate implementation timelines
    d. *"Will Tuesday morning at 9am work for our installation team to come in and begin the installation process?"*

Following the above procedure will help get your prospect's mind off their FUD (fear, uncertainty and doubt) over the money they just spent and shift the focus to enjoying the benefits.

Purposeful Professional Development

What makes a professional?

QUESTION: What is the difference between a sales rep and a *professional* sales rep?

ANSWER: Professionals are good at what they do and they know why. Professional Sales Reps make continuous learning a part of their process to improve sales. They learn, study and practice improving their Three A's.

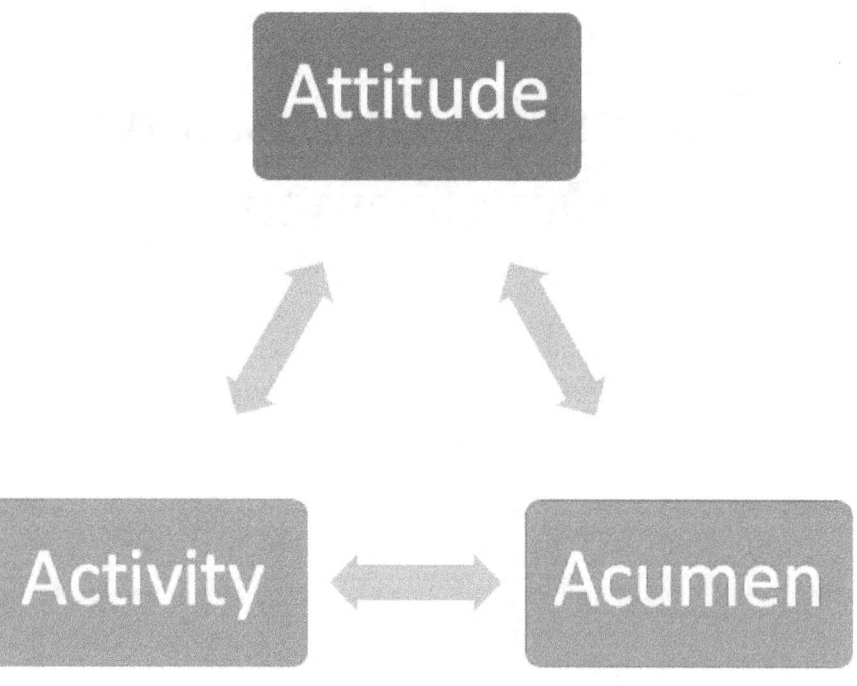

Purposeful Professional Development

What makes a professional?

ATTITUDE: They study and learn techniques that help them have a positive and confident attitude because they know that their success is 80% in their psychology and only 20% in knowing how and what to do.

ACTIVITY: Professional sales reps understand there is no magic bullet or formula when it comes to selling. At the end of the day, what brings them success is repeatedly performing the activities that lead to sales. Things like attending networking events, cold-calling, following-up, updating the CRM among others, are the only way that sales are made. NO ACTIVITY=NO SALE

ACUMEN: Professional sales reps are constant learners and practitioners. They look for new ideas and ways to improve the effectiveness of their activities. They study to learn ways to master their attitudes and skills, then they practice perfecting these skills so they become second nature.

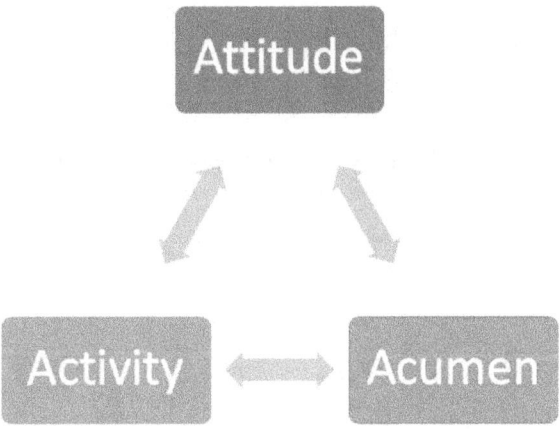

Purposeful Professional Development

<u>Training</u>

The initial and ongoing Sales Representative training and development should address these broad topics:

- Your company
- Your products/services
- Your industry
- The art and science of selling

Your completed SOS Package is the basis of your training program. You simply use the information you have assembled in this package as the training program. With your completed program you have a foundation for teaching information on:

- What your company is known for and what customers say about your company
- The features and benefits of your products/services
- Foundational procedures for selling your products at your company

You may want to provide additional information such as:

- Your competition
- How your company fits into the overall landscape of your industry
- Industry norms

Purposeful Professional Development

<u>On-Going Development</u>

Develop a plan with expectations for professional development. This could include:
- Regular sales training topics- how often and by whom?
- Required reading
- Sales Meetings
    - Sales reps take turns at each meeting teaching the other sales reps either:
        - Industry knowledge
        - Company/product knowledge
        - Professional selling knowledge

Evaluate "The Call": after each contact with a prospect, sales reps evaluate their performance in writing. This habit will allow sales reps to see trends and opportunities they may not have noticed had they not written down their evaluations.

- All sales reps are required to keep a journal and answer the following:
    - What went well?
    - Where could I improve?
    - What will I do next time?

Congratulations on completing SOS!

You've made it through the Sales Optimization System book. Did you implement as you went along, or did you just complete reading through SOS to get an idea on the steps you need to take in order to have an exceptional system for selling?

In my sales leadership and training career, I've discovered a basic truth among the many people involved at all levels of selling: owners, directors, managers, trainers, selling agents…

They all seem to be looking for the same thing. The elusive "Magic Bullet".

I'd like to dispel the myth of the "Magic Bullet". There is no secret formula to make everyone want to buy from you or your product. No matter how genuine and likable you are or how great your company and product/service are, there will be some who just don't need what you are selling, or they won't connect with you in a way that leads to a sale.

I've watched sales people get excited by a new method, believing it's the holy grail of selling, only to be dismayed and discouraged by their lack of overwhelming success. I see two things at play when this happens.

First, they try, whatever they learned, once or twice, and when they don't see any results, they abandon the effort. This is a fatal flaw when it comes to mastery. You simply won't get good at something if you don't practice and make it a part of your being.

Think about tying your shoes or riding a bike. When you first learned how to do these tasks, you had to really think about doing it. You were awkward, slow and made lots of mistakes. As you continued practicing, you became faster and more proficient. You can now do both of these activities without even consciously thinking of them.

If you had quit riding your bike after one or two attempts, you would have never gotten good at it. Same thing with sales techniques- they don't often come natural to us and we need to practice them in order to master them.

Secondly, when it comes to trying new sales strategies and techniques, we have unrealistic expectations on what it will mean to our selling success. We can fall into the trap of believing that if we implement and do everything just right, we'll be able to close every single sale.

Sales is a numbers game. Success isn't selling everyone. Think about it, not every product or service is right for you. Sometimes, you just don't connect or feel an affinity for something, even if many other people do. This is just human nature.

So, when considering the effectiveness and success you should get out of implementing a new strategy, like SOS, think about what would truly make a difference, and be realistic in your expectations.

SOS will improve your sales. You will most likely see some pretty amazing results if you haven't been strategically selling up to this point. However, you will NOT close every sale, nor will your sales reps.

What you can expect is to see improvements. Small, incremental improvements can have a staggering impact on your results though, and they have a compounding effect.

For instance, if you improved from one meeting to two meetings out of every one hundred cold calls, and everything else stays the same, you would double your sales.

If you then went from providing one proposal after every ten meetings with prospects to providing two proposals out of ten meetings, you'd again, double your sales. Combine these two and you'd quadruple your sales! Who wouldn't want to do that?

And, it doesn't stop there because there are countless other things you can do to improve your ratios at each step of the sales process. And, who says you have to go from one to two? You could go from one to five in any given area. In fact, when you see immediate improvements in one area, that may only be the tip of the iceberg, because as you get better from practice, your results will improve.

The moral of this is to stop searching for the magic bullets and see what is right in front of you. It's so obvious that it's easily missed. Sales success comes from doing the right activities, the right way, at the right time with the right attitude. Put all this together and you can't help but win!

I'm here to help. You can find many FREE tools and resources at www.salesoptimizationsystem.biz

Also, as a business owner who wants to bring on a team, you understand the need to delegate and leverage the time and talents of other people. You recognize your gifts and talents and know where your energies are best spent.

If implementing SOS isn't the best use of your time and energy, then consider hiring a Professional SOS Implementer who can help you get the results you want quickly.

Go to www.salesoptimizationsystem.biz and fill out the online form and one of our representatives will reach out to you and go over your options with you.

Sales Optimization System

Notes:

Sales Optimization System

Notes:

Sales Optimization System

Notes:

Sales Optimization System

Notes:

Sales Optimization System

Notes:

www.ingramcontent.com/pod-product-compliance
Lightning Source LLC
Chambersburg PA
CBHW070811220526
45466CB00002B/628